My First Acrostic

Leeds & Bradford

Edited by Angela Fairbrace

First published in Great Britain in 2009 by:

Young Writers
Remus House
Coltsfoot Drive
Peterborough
PE2 9JX
Telephone: 01733 890066
Website: www.youngwriters.co.uk

All Rights Reserved
© Copyright Contributors 2009
SB ISBN 978-1-84924-443-5

Foreword

The 'My First Acrostic' collection was developed by Young Writers specifically for Key Stage 1 children. The poetic form is simple, fun and gives the young poet a guideline to shape their ideas, yet at the same time leaves room for their imagination and creativity to begin to blossom.

Due to the young age of the entrants we have enjoyed rewarding their effort by including as many of the poems as possible. Our hope is that seeing their work in print will encourage the children to grow and develop their writing skills to become our poets of tomorrow.

Young Writers has been publishing children's poetry for over 19 years. Our aim is to nurture creativity in our children and young adults, to give them an interest in poetry and an outlet to express themselves. This latest collection will act as a milestone for the young poets and one that will be enjoyable to revisit again and again.

Contents

Bradford Moor Primary School, Bradford
Rafeena Bibi (7) 1
Jaahizah Hussain (6) 2
Samreena Arshad (7) 3
Uzair Afzal (7) 4
Amirah Nawaz (7) 5
Husnayn Amjad (7) 6
Aniq Mohammed (7) 7
Hassan Hussain (6) 8
Zainab Zaheer (6) 9
Deen Mohammed Gulfraz (5) 10
Hashir Mohammed (6) 11
Ayesha Ahmed (6) 12
Fatimah Khan (5) 13
Raja Shakir (6) 14
Ayesha Khan (6) 15
Laiba Hussain (6) 16
Khizar Akbar (6) 17
Subhaan Hamid (6) 18
Sehar Ali (5) 19
Hafsa Dawood (6) 20
Dawud Ghafar (6) 21
Hannah Khan (5) 22
Zunnera Hashmi (6) 23
Irma Ijaz (5) 24
Sabiha Mahnoor (5) 25
Sami Saeed (6) 26
Amaan Hussain & Hafsah Munir (6) .. 27
Hanzalah Aslam (5) 28

Bronte House School, Bradford
Matthew Shakespeare (6) 29
Daniel Glossop (5) 30
Zoe Ayres (5) 31
Sienna Sekhon (6) 32
Danyal Fiaz (6) 33
Willem Johnson (6) 34
Louis Anderson (5) 35
Simar Hare (6) 36
Grace Lancaster (7) 37
James Shoesmith-Evans (7) 38
Jaya Krishna (7) 39

Robert Albarda (7) 40
Laura Cavaliere (6) 41
Esther Bean (7) 42
Jake Fletcher-Stega (7) 43
Ellie Glossop (7) 44
Ellie Young (6) 45
Zara Butt (7) 46
Rohan Patel (6) 47
Thomas Pratt (6) 48
Benjamin O'Shea (7) 49
Flora Lawson (6) 50
Molly Bradshaw (7) 51
Adam Ramsay (6) 52
Naveena Amrat (6) 53
Owen Maiden-Lumb (5) 54
Olivia Pringle (5) 55
Abbie Hinchliffe (5) 56
Louis Tarleton (5) 57
Ned Hawker (6) 58
Jude Hall (6) 59
Oscar Bowling (5) 60
Tayler Boothroyd (6) 61

Byron Primary School, Bradford
Mohammed Zubhir (7) 62
Iqrah Usman (7) 63
Hafizur Rahman (7) 64
Anisha Khaliq (6) 65
Habiba Khalifa (7) 66
Aminah Kauser (7) 67
Imaan Hussain (7) 68
Adnan Hassan (7) 69
Nazim Thamid Choudhury (7) 70
Saliha Kauser 71
Wahaaj Hasnain Ahmed (7) 72
Umar Taj (7) 73
Nafeesa Iqball (7) 74
Anisha Hussain (7) 75
Fizzah Khalifa (6) 76
Haiqa Salim (7) 77
Zaynah Khan (7) 78
Hanfia Khan (7) 79
Taybah Khan (7) 80

Yumn Batool (7) 81	Brandon Johnson (6) 125
Zahra Choudhry (7) 82	Jacob Thewlis (5) 126
Ammarah Bibi (7) 83	Sofia Downie Hullah (6) 127
Faizah Bano (6) 84	Curtis Fox (5) 128
Khuzeema Arshad (7) 85	Matilda Peat (5) 129
Adeeb Hussain (7) 86	Elizabeth Ketteringham (6) 130
Musfira Imran (6) 87	Ellie Fox (6) 131
Hafsah Sultana (7) 88	Lydia Gill (6) 132
Muhibur Rahman (7) 89	Meena Blair (6) 133
	Bethany Allen (6) 134

Churwell Primary School, Morley

Lapage Primary School, Bradford

Spencer Walton (5) 90	Aishah Hussain (6) 135
Shannon Dawson (6) 91	Malikah Ahmed (6) 136
Lenah Ahmed (6) 92	Tashnia Begum (6) 137
Olivia Reah (5) 93	Zanab Razwan (6) 138
Jordan Holmes (6) 94	Qurratulayn Kazmi (6) 139
Harris Brereton (5) 95	Amaan Ali Maryam (5) 140
Ashley Metcalf (6) 96	Loeeza Maryam (5) 141
Jayden Hills (5) 97	Afia Yasmin Khan (6) 142
Charlie Green (5) 98	
Emma Skitt (5) 99	**Oakwood Primary School, Leeds**
Elanya Farrell (6) 100	Liam Ralph (6) 143
Japnbir Kour (6) 101	Shyla Keeble (6) 144
Mya Seehra (5) 102	Billy Griffin (6) 145
Joe Matthews (5) 103	Ibrahim Mohammed (6) 146
Riya Patel (6) 104	Paige Smith (6) 147
Macy Prentice (6) 105	Ella McNalus (5) 148
Kieran Gunn (6) 106	Aaron Pitts-Smith (6) 149
Nathan Boote (6) 107	Zeshan Aziz 150
Joseph Pyett (5) 108	Farai Kavuru (6) 151
Sophie Anderson (5) 109	
Georgia Bennett (6) 110	**SS Peter & Paul RC Primary School, Yeadon**
Harry Germaine (6) 111	
Darcy Elam (6) 112	Harry Emmott (7) 152
Charley Wilson (6) 113	William Davy (7) 153
Ethan Booth (5) 114	Adanna Okonofua (6) 154
Euan Henderson (6) 115	Joseph Langley (7) 155
Lily Sissons (6) 116	Jack Hazlegreaves (7) 156
Evan Roper (6) 117	Bethany Broadbent (6) 157
Harry Wiffen (6) 118	May Gavin (7) 158
Aaron Sykes (6) 119	Niamh Way (7) 159
Chloe Stead (6) 120	Holly Mifsud (7) 160
Amelie Chapagnon (6) 121	Rory Folan (6) 161
Mason Pattison (5) 122	
Max Dickinson (6) 123	**St Anthony's Catholic Primary School, Beeston**
Alicia Patnelli (6) 124	Ebony Clark (6) 162

Caitlin Deacon (6) 163
Elliot O'Reilly (7) 164
Joshua Staniland (7) 165
Émer Thompson (7) 166
Ellie-Anne Thompson (6) 167
Ellie Gawthorpe (6) 168
Evie Plews (7) 169
Oliver Spoors (7) 170
Elizabeth Todd (7) 171
Lucas Lee (7) 172
Joseph Maloney (7) 173
Patrick Hirsch (7) 174

St Francis' Catholic Primary School, Morley
Casey Lee (6) 175
Patrick Richardson (7) 176
Victoria Massey (5) 177
Lucas Ottley (5) 178
Lauren Wilson (5) 179
Harry Bussey (5) 180
Fawn Goodwin (7) 181
Olivia Turner (7) 182
Fletcher Trueman (6) 183
Amy Atkin (7) 184

Shadwell Primary School, Shadwell
Corey Franks (6) 185
Charles Fenwick (5) 186
Polly Wearmouth (6) 187
Ruby Fullman (5) 188
Maddie Wood (6) 189
Harry Fenwick (5) 190
Megan Davis (6) 191
Daniel Coates (6) 192
Maisie Hanna Wood 193
Imogen Bowman (6) 194
Amber Webb (6) 195
Ali Naim 196

The Poems

My First Acrostic - Leeds & Bradford

Rafeena

R abbits I like
A nd
F urry cats
E lephants enjoying themselves
E at lots of food
N uts to eat
A n animal I like is a zebra.

Rafeena Bibi (7)
Bradford Moor Primary School, Bradford

Jaahizah

J aahizah likes playing with her toys
A nts crawl in my garden
A rmaan is my brother's name
H anisha is my sister
I like ice cream
Z oos are my favourite place
A pples are sweet
H ana is my new baby sister.

Jaahizah Hussain (6)
Bradford Moor Primary School, Bradford

My First Acrostic - Leeds & Bradford

Samreena

S wimming is my favourite exercise
A car was called a Buggatti
M yra is playing with Aysha
R unning makes your heart beat
E at healthy food
E very time I want ice cream
N obody makes me laugh when they are not being funny
A t dinner I want jacket potatoes.

Samreena Arshad (7)
Bradford Moor Primary School, Bradford

Uzair

U mbrella will keep me dry
Z ebras I like because they have stripes
A wild animal I like because they are always angry
I play with my brother
R unning for exercise.

Uzair Afzal (7)
Bradford Moor Primary School, Bradford

My First Acrostic - Leeds & Bradford

Amirah Nawaz

A mirah is 7 years old
M orning is nice and bright
I undertstand my school rules
R ainbows are bright and nice
A nd I like brown ponies
H elps people in class, that is why I do not get my name on the board

N ever breaks the school rules
A nam is my best, best friend
W e always help each other
A lways good
Z zzzzz!

Amirah Nawaz (7)
Bradford Moor Primary School, Bradford

Husnayn Amjad

H usnayn is 7 years old
U se me to spell hard words for you
S omebody needs help, I'm off there
N obody annoys me
A na's taught me to skip
Y ou're my best friend
N ever been naughty

A dentist is a tooth's best friend
M y favourite colours are gold and silver
' J oe is a frog,' is my favourite song
A nd 'What a beast' is my other favourite song
D o I listen?

Husnayn Amjad (7)
Bradford Moor Primary School, Bradford

My First Acrostic - Leeds & Bradford

Aniq

A niq is 7 years old
N ever breaks the rules - almost!
I s good at football
Q uickly he runs around the playground.

Aniq Mohammed (7)
Bradford Moor Primary School, Bradford

Lion

L ikes to eat meat
I n the jungle
O n the grass
N asty.

Hassan Hussain (6)
Bradford Moor Primary School, Bradford

My First Acrostic - Leeds & Bradford

Lion

L ion eating meat
I n the jungle
O n the log
N ever touch his teeth.

Zainab Zaheer (6)
Bradford Moor Primary School, Bradford

Lion

L ions roar
I n Africa
O n the tree
N ever look at the lion's teeth.

Deen Mohammed Gulfraz (5)
Bradford Moor Primary School, Bradford

My First Acrostic - Leeds & Bradford

Lion

L ion eats grass
I n the jungle
O n the tree
N ever touch.

Hashir Mohammed (6)
Bradford Moor Primary School, Bradford

Rhino

R osy goes to the park
H ot, sunny day
I nk has run out
N o doubt, turn off the light
O nce the rhino met a dog.

Ayesha Ahmed (6)
Bradford Moor Primary School, Bradford

Elephant

E lephants eat lollipops
L ikes a giraffe
E lephants are nice
P erfect in every way
H e sings
A t all the others from
N ow
T ill they say *stop!*

Fatimah Khan (5)
Bradford Moor Primary School, Bradford

Snake

S nake
N obody to chase
A ll by himself
K ing of the snakes
E ating his chocolate cake.

Raja Shakir (6)
Bradford Moor Primary School, Bradford

My First Acrostic - Leeds & Bradford

Elephant

E lephants eat grass
L ove peanuts
E aster eggs
P aint the fence
H ide in the water
A nts in their pants
N ice to see you
T ry to get up.

Ayesha Khan (6)
Bradford Moor Primary School, Bradford

Cheetahs

C hocolate mousse is his favourite
H e is drinking milk
E very day
E normous black spots
T urning into red
A doctor, a doctor!
'H elp, my tummy is hurting!'
S aid the fluffy cheetah.

Laiba Hussain (6)
Bradford Moor Primary School, Bradford

My First Acrostic - Leeds & Bradford

Tiger

T iger running to the park
I roning his fur
G rowling on the way
E ating chocolate
R unning back home.

Khizar Akbar (6)
Bradford Moor Primary School, Bradford

Snake

S melly snake
N apping in the sea
A ngry snake
K ing of the world at the
E nd of the day.

Subhaan Hamid (6)
Bradford Moor Primary School, Bradford

My First Acrostic - Leeds & Bradford

Snake

S low snake
N aughty snake
A ngry snake
K ing snake
E veryone's friend.

Sehar Ali (5)
Bradford Moor Primary School, Bradford

Rhino

R uns fast
H armless in the water
I t's so big
N ervous
O n the logs.

Hafsa Dawood (6)
Bradford Moor Primary School, Bradford

My First Acrostic - Leeds & Bradford

Cheetah

C ounts its notes
H e saved his mum
E veryone is on the floor
E ating chocolate
T oo many sweets
A ll feel sick
H ave to go home.

Dawud Ghafar (6)
Bradford Moor Primary School, Bradford

Lion

L ion has lots of teeth
I t has ants in its pants
O n Wednesday
N obody to play with.

Hannah Khan (5)
Bradford Moor Primary School, Bradford

My First Acrostic - Leeds & Bradford

Giraffe

G iant giraffe
I n the jungle
R unning through the plants
A nts in his pants
F rightening all the
F ish
E very day.

Zunnera Hashmi (6)
Bradford Moor Primary School, Bradford

Cheetahs

C hocolate mousse is his favourite
H e is eating grass
E very day
E normous black spots
T urning into red
A doctor, a doctor,
'**H** elp me, my tummy is hurting,'
S aid the fluffy cheetah.

Irma Ijaz (5)
Bradford Moor Primary School, Bradford

My First Acrostic - Leeds & Bradford

Bears

B aboon was playing with the bears
E ggs were falling from the tree
A ngry was the baboon
R acing his friends
S nakes in his pants.

Sabiha Mahnoor (5)
Bradford Moor Primary School, Bradford

Cheetahs

C hocolate mousse is his favourite
H e is cheating
E very day
E normous black spots
T urning into yellow
A doctor came to his house
'**H** elp me, my tummy is hurting,'
S aid the gigantic cheetah.

Sami Saeed (6)
Bradford Moor Primary School, Bradford

My First Acrostic - Leeds & Bradford

Snake

S lithery snake
N obody to chase
A ll by himself
K ing of the snakes
E ating his chocolate cake.

Amaan Hussain & Hafsah Munir (6)
Bradford Moor Primary School, Bradford

Cheetahs

C hocolate mousse is his favourite
H e is running fast
E very day
E normous black spots
T urning into red
A doctor, a doctor
'**H** elp me, my tummy is hurting,'
S aid the fluffy cheetah.

Hanzalah Aslam (5)
Bradford Moor Primary School, Bradford

My First Acrostic - Leeds & Bradford

Matthew

Milk is my favourite drink
Apples are my favourite fruit
Tennis is fun to play
Tigers are my best animal
Holiday is my best year
Eyes are brown
Weather is sunny today.

Matthew Shakespeare (6)
Bronte House School, Bradford

Daniel

Diggers are my best trucks
Apples are my favourite fruit
Night is when I like to sleep
I like bouncing on the trampoline
Elephants are my favourite
Light is when I play.

Daniel Glossop (5)
Bronte House School, Bradford

My First Acrostic - Leeds & Bradford

Zoe

Z ebras are my favourite
O scar is very, very funny
E llen is my best friend.

Zoe Ayres (5)
Bronte House School, Bradford

Sienna

S leeping at home
I n the night
E yes are brown
N ight is dark
N ecklaces have love hearts
A pples are yummy.

Sienna Sekhon (6)
Bronte House School, Bradford

My First Acrostic - Leeds & Bradford

Danyal

D an is my swimming teacher
A lex is funny
N ice football
Y o-yo is my favourite toy
A had is my best friend
L ouis is my favourite friend.

Danyal Fiaz (6)
Bronte House School, Bradford

Willem

Water is my favourite
I like to make igloos
L ike going on holiday
L ovely Mummy
E than is my friend
M y new baby, soon.

Willem Johnson (6)
Bronte House School, Bradford

My First Acrostic - Leeds & Bradford

Louis

L ions are my favourite
O ranges are nice to eat
U mbrellas keep me dry from the rain
'I ncredibles' I like to watch
S ummer is my sister.

Louis Anderson (5)
Bronte House School, Bradford

Simar

S eem happy
I f I am happy I will play
M y friends are the best
A rjun is my brother
R oom is red.

Simar Hare (6)
Bronte House School, Bradford

My First Acrostic - Leeds & Bradford

Find Out About Grace

G us used to be my pet dog
R acing around all day long - that's Grace
A pple is my favourite fruit
C asper is the name of my pet fish
E sther is my best friend.

Grace Lancaster (7)
Bronte House School, Bradford

The Cool Poem

J ames loves swimming, especially breaststroke
A chocolate pudding is my favourite pudding
M y friends are very nice to me and they help me
E very day I work hard and try my best
S inging is very enjoyable for me.

James Shoesmith-Evans (7)
Bronte House School, Bradford

Jaya's Poem

J uice is my favourite drink
A spider is scary to me
Y ellow is my favourite colour
A limo is my favourite car.

Jaya Krishna (7)
Bronte House School, Bradford

A Poem About Me!

R obert likes to work and play Star Wars

O ranges he likes, blueberries he hates

B irthday is on the 30th of June

E ric is his friend

R obert's favourite land is America

T o his nose to his chin, he likes football.

Robert Albarda (7)
Bronte House School, Bradford

My First Acrostic - Leeds & Bradford

Poetry All About Me

L earning every day, fun along the way
A my, my sister, puts a smile on my face
U mbrellas keep me dry, when rain comes from the sky
R unning like the wind is everyone but me
A n ice cream stops my fears, when I'm in tears.

Laura Cavaliere (6)
Bronte House School, Bradford

Fabulous Poem

E sther has lots of friends at school
S cience is my favourite subject
T uesday is my favourite day because I go to gymnastics
H olidays are fun for me
E verybody knows I am on the school council
R ainbows make me happy because they're beautiful.

Esther Bean (7)
Bronte House School, Bradford

My First Acrostic - Leeds & Bradford

Friends Poem

J ake likes cake for dessert
A n apple is Jake's favourite
K icking a football in the goal
E lliot lives next door but one

S ometimes when Mum's not looking, I eat chocolate
T alking to everyone in Year Two
E xcited when his friends are here
' G oal!' I shout when Man U score
A banana is my least favourite fruit.

Jake Fletcher-Stega (7)
Bronte House School, Bradford

The Pretty Poem

E xcellent people her friends really are
L ining up her knitting very neat
L eaping around in the air all day
I mpossible to stop, she just carries on
E llie the elephant is what she calls herself

G lossop is her last name
L ooping around in the air is her game
O livia is her sister's name
S he squeals all day and night
S creaming and giving everyone a headache
O nions she really hates
P ainting pots and putting them to dry is her favourite thing to do.

Ellie Glossop (7)
Bronte House School, Bradford

My First Acrostic - Leeds & Bradford

Me!

E normous writing is my favourite type of writing
L earning every week is great
L iteracy is my favourite lesson
I sabella is my best friend
E nergetic is not my type.

Ellie Young (6)
Bronte House School, Bradford

All About Me

Zigzag Zara across the road

Apperley Bridge is where I live

Riding my bike is my favourite hobby

Always laughing here and there

Bouncing along I go

Under a bright blue sky

Tiny me skipping along

To and fro I go.

Zara Butt (7)
Bronte House School, Bradford

All About Me

R iding with my sisters
O n the road we go
H emal goes to university in the car
A nd my dad takes me to the park
N early every day I play football.

Rohan Patel (6)
Bronte House School, Bradford

All About Me

Talking boy
Happy playing football
One giddy boy
Messy Thomas
A laughing boy
Soccer is my best sport

Perfect Thomas
Racing boy
Amazing Thomas
Tickling boy
Thomas has seen Big Ben!

Thomas Pratt (6)
Bronte House School, Bradford

My First Acrostic - Leeds & Bradford

All About Me

B rave at football
E ndless at working
N ice to people
J olly wally
A wesome at things
M assive Bejamin
I nterested in history
N ice friend

O nly ever nice
S leepy Benjamin
H appy all the time
E verything's easy
A merican fan.

Benjamin O'Shea (7)
Bronte House School, Bradford

All About Me

F riendly to everyone
L ovely every day
O ne happy girl
R osy cheeks
A lways kind

L aughing with Molly
A kind sister
W orking hard
S illy Flora
O nly one Flora
N ice piano playing.

Flora Lawson (6)
Bronte House School, Bradford

My First Acrostic - Leeds & Bradford

All About Me

Musical with my flute
One happy girl
Lovely every day
Laughing with my friends
Young and beautiful

Big sister to my little brother
Rosy cheeks every day
All alone at night
Dancing in my bedroom
Silly with my big brother
Happy every day
Always only one Molly in the class
Works hard every day.

Molly Bradshaw (7)
Bronte House School, Bradford

All About Me

A lways ready to work
D iving is what I want to learn
A nd I like to play in my house
M y friend is called Joe

R eally good every day
A kind person
M y favourite colour is red
S ometimes I go to Beavers
A m a good friend
Y ou could play Star Wars with me.

Adam Ramsay (6)
Bronte House School, Bradford

My First Acrostic - Leeds & Bradford

Naveena

N aveena is my name
A bbie is my friend
V iolet is one of my favourite colours
E aster eggs are yummy
E very Monday I have a violin lesson
N ovember is the month of my birthday
A lton Towers is a fun place to go.

Naveena Amrat (6)
Bronte House School, Bradford

Owen

O scar is my best friend
W inning a competition would be fun
E very night I read books
N ed is a boy in my class.

Owen Maiden-Lumb (5)
Bronte House School, Bradford

My First Acrostic - Leeds & Bradford

Olivia

O livia is my name
L ee is my daddy
I like playing with my sister
V iolet is my favourite colour
I have a little sister called Sadie
A nn is my grandma.

Olivia Pringle (5)
Bronte House School, Bradford

Abbie

A bbie is my name
B utterflies are my favourite animal
B lue is the colour of my eyes
I can ride my two-wheeled bike
E vie is my best friend.

Abbie Hinchliffe (5)
Bronte House School, Bradford

Louis

L ouis is my name
O range is my favourite fruit
U pstairs is where my classroom is
I love chocolate
S uzie is my mummy's name.

Louis Tarleton (5)
Bronte House School, Bradford

Ned

N ed is my name
E agles are my favourite animal
D ad is a dentist.

Ned Hawker (6)
Bronte House School, Bradford

My First Acrostic - Leeds & Bradford

Jude

J ude is my name
U nder the sea is an excellent place to be
D ogs are my favourite pet
E veryone is my friend.

Jude Hall (6)
Bronte House School, Bradford

Oscar

O scar is my name
S occer is my favourite sport
C harlie is my daddy
A nya is my favourite cousin
R iding on my bike is fun.

Oscar Bowling (5)
Bronte House School, Bradford

My First Acrostic - Leeds & Bradford

Tayler

T ayler is my name
A monkey is my favourite animal
Y is the third letter of my name
L issel is my friend
E ating sweets is great
R ed is my favourite colour.

Tayler Boothroyd (6)
Bronte House School, Bradford

All About Me

Z ero plus 7 years old
U ses the PlayStation every time
B est at football
H ard work I do every time
I like playing on my bike
R emember too many things in my brain.

Mohammed Zubhir (7)
Byron Primary School, Bradford

My First Acrostic - Leeds & Bradford

All About Me

I am 7 years old
Quite loud
Red and pink are my favourite colours
Always I am naughty
Has glasses.

Use tissues when I sneeze
Says naughty stuff
Might hit someone walking past
Am a good artist
Never am good.

Iqrah Usman (7)
Byron Primary School, Bradford

All About Me

H ard-working and good
A lways fast in racing
F riend of Zubhir
I am good at football
Z ero plus 7 years old
U ses trainers
R emembers everything.

Hafizur Rahman (7)
Byron Primary School, Bradford

My First Acrostic - Leeds & Bradford

All About Me

A lways reads books.
N ever got my name in the book this half-term.
I maan is my friend.
S chool is fun.
H aleema is my friend.
A lways go to mosque except on Saturday and Sunday.

Anisha Khaliq (6)
Byron Primary School, Bradford

All About Me

H abiba has a little sister
A lways forgets stuff
B est at drawing
I am seven years old
B est at skipping
A lways plays with people.

Habiba Khalifa (7)
Byron Primary School, Bradford

All About Me

A lways reads books
M ight fiddle sometimes
I have black hair
N ever stops reading books
A lways eats fruit
H as got cuddly teddies.

Aminah Kauser (7)
Byron Primary School, Bradford

All About Me

I am 7 years old

M y sister copies me

A pple is my favourite fruit

A mal is my sister

N ice person

H ussain is my second name

U sually I am good

S ometimes I forget my homework

S ahialal is my cousin

A nisha is my friend

I like skipping

N ever fights.

Imaan Hussain (7)
Byron Primary School, Bradford

My First Acrostic - Leeds & Bradford

All About Me

A lways likes to do work in school
D oesn't kick, swear, fight, scratch or hit people
N ever ever had a severe warning in Byron School
A lways listens the first time teachers say in Byron School
N ever eats too much food.

H as a shop
A lways does good paintings
S ays good stuff
S ometimes is left-handed but often is right-handed
A lways does good work
N ot had his name in the book this half-term or last half-term.

Adnan Hassan (7)
Byron Primary School, Bradford

All About Me

T elevision has my favourite cartoons
H elicopters are my favourite toys
A m always playing with my speedboat
M y mum gets lollipops from the ice cream van
I play with my cousin
D o my homework.

Nazim Thamid Choudhury (7)
Byron Primary School, Bradford

My First Acrostic - Leeds & Bradford

All About Me

Sometimes I tell the truth and don't shout at people
Always scared of thunder outside
Lolly is my favourite sweet
I am scared of the dark and I like to watch cartoons on TV
Holidays are fun because we don't have to go to school
or mosque and we get to play outside every day
Always read a book quietly.

Saliha Kauser
Byron Primary School, Bradford

All About Me

Water is very good for me
A pple is my favourite fruit
H as good grades
A lways I learn reading
A ll the time I try hard
J eans are my favourite clothes.

Wahaaj Hasnain Ahmed (7)
Byron Primary School, Bradford

My First Acrostic - Leeds & Bradford

All About Me

U ses lots of stuff to make things
M ostly I help my friends
A lways I say good things about my friends
R espect all of the teachers.

Umar Taj (7)
Byron Primary School, Bradford

All About Me

N afeesa is naughty sometimes
A lways forget stuff
F ood is my favourite
E lephant is my favourite animal
E ating healthy food is good
S ometimes I listen
A lways I play at home.

Nafeesa Iqball (7)
Byron Primary School, Bradford

My First Acrostic - Leeds & Bradford

All About Me

A lways do nice writing
N ever lies
I sn't naughty
S ays nice things
H as glasses
A lways has friends

Anisha Hussain (7)
Byron Primary School, Bradford

All About Me

F ruit is my favourite
I like monkeys on TV
'Z ap' is my favourite film
Z ebra is my favourite animal
A lways I play with my friends
H orse is my best toy.

Fizzah Khalifa (6)
Byron Primary School, Bradford

My First Acrostic - Leeds & Bradford

All About Me

H aiqa always tries to work hard and has to go to the doctors
A pples are my favourite fruit
I always play with my favourite best friends
Q uiet always at school and mosque
A ll my friends are the best, especially my parents and teachers.

Haiqa Salim (7)
Byron Primary School, Bradford

All About Me

Z ap Rap is my favourite cartoon
A lways be good
Y ummy beans are my favourite
N ever talk on the carpet
A lways do the work
H ave a good memory.

Zaynah Khan (7)
Byron Primary School, Bradford

My First Acrostic - Leeds & Bradford

All About Me

H anfia is in the top group
A ll my friends try very hard
N ative Deen is my favourite hymn and it is by Zain Bhikha
F unfair is in mosque on Sunday
I love the team Liverpool FC in football
A pples are my best fruit.

Hanfia Khan (7)
Byron Primary School, Bradford

About Taybah

T ry to get my work right
A nd I am clean
Y our best friend is Yumn
B ecause she is fun
A nd I help people when they are stuck
H as a nice class

K ind
H elpful when the teacher needs me to be
A lways good
N ever bad.

Taybah Khan (7)
Byron Primary School, Bradford

My First Acrostic - Leeds & Bradford

About Yumn

Y our best friend is Taybah
U ses the school rules
M ight be silly sometimes
N ever swears

B est at reading
A lways is hard-working
T ries to be in the happy book
O ften is sensible
O ften is fit and healthy
L oves her cat.

Yumn Batool (7)
Byron Primary School, Bradford

About Zahra

Z ahra is a good girl
A lways comes to school
H as a friend called Zulikha
R emembers when she was little
A lways tries to be a good girl.

Zahra Choudhry (7)
Byron Primary School, Bradford

My First Acrostic - Leeds & Bradford

About Ammarah

A lways happy
M y best friend is Zulikha
M ight be sad sometimes
A lways like playing with my friends
R emembers always to be good
A lways remember what I have to do
H onest and polite.

Ammarah Bibi (7)
Byron Primary School, Bradford

About Faizah

F aizah is short
A lways sensible on the carpet
I sn't bad, always happy
Z ig-zags when running in the playground
A m friendly and nice
H as a nice time in the playground.

Faizah Bano (6)
Byron Primary School, Bradford

My First Acrostic - Leeds & Bradford

About Khuzeema

K huzeema is tall
H as a sister
U rooj is my friend
Z ahra is in my class
E xcellent at literacy
E specially kind
M ight be sensible
A nd I am kind.

Khuzeema Arshad (7)
Byron Primary School, Bradford

About Adeeb

A good friend
D oes not get silly
E ats healthy things
E xtra chatty
B est at reading.

Adeeb Hussain (7)
Byron Primary School, Bradford

My First Acrostic - Leeds & Bradford

About Musfira

M ight boss people
U ses pencils to write
S ometimes shouts
F riends with Haiqa
I go to the mosque
R aises money at school
A lot of friends.

Musfira Imran (6)
Byron Primary School, Bradford

About Hafsah

H i, I am pretty
A nd I am funny
F riendly and kind
S ometimes I get angry
A nd I am good
H ave I got friends?

S ometimes I get to be the helper
U rooj is my best friend
L olly is my favourite thing
T ry to work hard
A nd I am always happy
N ever break the rules
A nd never swear.

Hafsah Sultana (7)
Byron Primary School, Bradford

My First Acrostic - Leeds & Bradford

About Muhibur

M uhibur is sensible
U ses things to work
H as some books at home
I am not a fast writer
B est at listening
U ses a pencil to work
R emembers things that happened in nursery.

Muhibur Rahman (7)
Byron Primary School, Bradford

Dragon

D eep in a dark, gloomy cave
R evolting
A mazing
G littering, glittering
O ld
N ails.

Spencer Walton (5)
Churwell Primary School, Morley

My First Acrostic - Leeds & Bradford

Dragon

D ark, gloomy caves are where you will find a dragon
R ed scales on its body
A mazing dragon
G littering eyes that sparkle
O pen mouth with razor-sharp teeth
N esting his golden things in there.

Shannon Dawson (6)
Churwell Primary School, Morley

Dragons

D angerous fiery breath coming out of his mouth

R ough, red, spiky scales on his back

A mazing knights can kill dragons

G olden, glittery, glowing treasure

O ily, blue, oval eyes on his face

N oisy dragons roaring over the hills in their spooky, gloomy cave.

Lenah Ahmed (6)
Churwell Primary School, Morley

Dragon

D azzling, scaly, yellow skin
R ed flaming fire coming from the hill
A crobatic legs that can run 200 miles
G olden skin shines bright
O val eyes that stare at you
N ails as long as his tail.

Olivia Reah (5)
Churwell Primary School, Morley

Dragon

D eafening roars across the hills
R oaring across the hills
A mazing acrobatic dragon can fly
G olden caves are where dragons live
O pen their mouths is what dragons do when they are hungry
N asty dragon.

Jordan Holmes (6)
Churwell Primary School, Morley

My First Acrostic - Leeds & Bradford

Dragon

D eep, gloomy cave
R azor sharp teeth
A dventurous dragon
G iant dragon
O ld dagon
N asty dragon.

Harris Brereton (5)
Churwell Primary School, Morley

Dragon

D eep in a lava-hot volcano

R evolting dragons can breathe hot flames

A dventurous

G littering dragons

O pen mouth

N asty dragons.

Ashley Metcalf (6)
Churwell Primary School, Morley

My First Acrostic - Leeds & Bradford

Dragon

D azzling scales cover the dragon's back
R ed body with red eyes
A mazing sharp, clean teeth
G littering treasure he collects every day
O pen mouth with fiery flames coming out
N asty temper with a loud roar.

Jayden Hills (5)
Churwell Primary School, Morley

Dragon

D angerous and fierce

R ed skin

A crobat

G o back to your gloomy cave

O pen mouth

N asty.

Charlie Green (5)
Churwell Primary School, Morley

My First Acrostic - Leeds & Bradford

Dragon

D angerous
R azor-sharp teeth
A sh
G reat
O pen mouth
N asty.

Emma Skitt (5)
Churwell Primary School, Morley

Dragon

D angerous and noisy
R oaring loud as it goes over the hill
A mazing dragon
G rowling as loud
O pening mouth with razor-sharp teeth
N asty dragon.

Elanya Farrell (6)
Churwell Primary School, Morley

My First Acrostic - Leeds & Bradford

Dragon

D eep in a forest there is a dark, scary, red dragon
R oaring loud
A crobats because they swing their wings
G olden treasure
O val eyes and nose
N asty dragon with sharp nails.

Japnbir Kour (6)
Churwell Primary School, Morley

Dragon

D ragons' teeth bite you
R eally red dragon
A dragon is as cold as ice
G reat
O ld
N ails.

Mya Seehra (5)
Churwell Primary School, Morley

My First Acrostic - Leeds & Bradford

Dragon

D ragons are in dark caves
R ough over the hill
A crobatic and adventurous
G reat scaly skin
O pen mouth
N asty dragon in a cave.

Joe Matthews (5)
Churwell Primary School, Morley

Dragon

D ark, hot, growling dragon roaring against other people
R evolting red dragon making lots and lots of noise
A dventurous, amazing dragon peeking in the cave
G olden, glittery, amazing treasure deep in the cave
O ld dragon in the pink cave
N ails black and dirty and he is very nasty.

Riya Patel (6)
Churwell Primary School, Morley

My First Acrostic - Leeds & Bradford

Dragon

D angerous dragon

R azor-sharp claws

A crobatic dragon

G lowing cave

O ld dragon

N est for a dragon.

Macy Prentice (6)
Churwell Primary School, Morley

Dragon

D angerous dark cave

R ed evil eyes

A mazing flying abilities

G olden sparkling treasure

O ld dragons die

N est full of eggs.

Kieran Gunn (6)
Churwell Primary School, Morley

My First Acrostic - Leeds & Bradford

Dragon

D angerous and very ferocious
R azor-sharp teeth that can eat you up"
A crobatic when they are turning round and round
G iant and growling as they fly
O pen fire-breathing mouth
N oisy, mighty roars coming out of its mouth.

Nathan Boote (6)
Churwell Primary School, Morley

Dragon

D ark, gloomy cave

R ed fire

A crobatic dragon

G littery cave

O ld, grumpy dragon

N asty, mean dragon.

Joseph Pyett (5)
Churwell Primary School, Morley

My First Acrostic - Leeds & Bradford

Dragon

D angerous, fierce, ferocious dragon
R ed-hot fiery breath coming from the dragon's mouth
A ngry dragon coming to eat you!
G loomy, dark, silly, revolting cave
O n the way a dragon is finding your treasure
N asty, naughty dragon never came back.

Sophie Anderson (5)
Churwell Primary School, Morley

Dragon

D ark, gloomy caves are where you can see dragons
R ed fire-breathing out of the dragon's mouth
A mazing things that dragons do when they are flying
G olden sparkling treasure that dragons hide
O ld dragons teeth are razor-sharp
N oisy dragons say *roar!*

Georgia Bennett (6)
Churwell Primary School, Morley

My First Acrostic - Leeds & Bradford

Dragon

D eafening roars over the hills and far away

R ough red scales on the dragon

A mazing, gold, glittery treasure under his tail

G reat horses with knights on them ride to fight him

O val eyes looking at the knight, kill it

N ever come alive again, dragon.

Harry Germaine (6)
Churwell Primary School, Morley

Dragons

D ragons are very mischievous
R eally scary
A ngry dragons are strong and powerful
G entle or not
O pen their mouths as wide as a head
N asty dragons are powerful
S ly dragons can try to fit in your house.

Darcy Elam (6)
Churwell Primary School, Morley

My First Acrostic - Leeds & Bradford

Dragons

D angerous creatures
R avenous giants
A ble to gobble you up!
G laring, his eyes light up
O bey him or he will eat you!
N asty, horrible dragon
S cary dragons.

Charley Wilson (6)
Churwell Primary School, Morley

Dragons

D angerous dragons are
R eally loud
A nd breathe fire
G reat at terrifying people
O ften horrifying
N ever friendly
S cary as a monster.

Ethan Booth (5)
Churwell Primary School, Morley

My First Acrostic - Leeds & Bradford

Dragon

D angerous creatures
R avenous giants
A bout to gobble you up!
G laring are his eyes
O bey him or he will eat you
N asty
S tay away.

Euan Henderson (6)
Churwell Primary School, Morley

Dragons

D angerous dragons breathe fire
R avenous creatures they are
A nd very scary
G obble you up
O h they just want to eat you
N o one likes a dragon
S tay away!

Lily Sissons (6)
Churwell Primary School, Morley

My First Acrostic - Leeds & Bradford

Dragons

D angerous dragons

R avenous dragons

A nd very scary and fierce

G reedy dragons

O ften fierce

N ever go near them

S tay away!

Evan Roper (6)
Churwell Primary School, Morley

Dragons

D angerous dragons breathe fire
R avenous they are
A nd breathe fire
G reat at scaring people
O ften scary
N ever normal
S tay away!

Harry Wiffen (6)
Churwell Primary School, Morley

My First Acrostic - Leeds & Bradford

Dragons

D ragons are dangerous
R oar loudly
A nd breathe fire
G reat creatures
O bviously scary
N o dragon is nice
S ee the dragon breathe fire.

Aaron Sykes (6)
Churwell Primary School, Morley

Dragons

D angerous they are
R oar loudly they do
A nd evil creatures they are
G reat they are not
O ften horrible
N ever good
S tay away!

Chloe Stead (6)
Churwell Primary School, Morley

My First Acrostic - Leeds & Bradford

Dragons

D angerous dragons fight
R eally ravenous
A nd very petrifying
G entle – *not!*
O dd animals
N asty a lot
S tay away all the time!

Amelie Chapagnon (6)
Churwell Primary School, Morley

Dragons

D angerous creatures
R avenous giants
A ble to gobble you up
G laring his eyes
O bey him or he will eat you up
N asty dragon
S cary, frightening dragon.

Mason Pattison (5)
Churwell Primary School, Morley

My First Acrostic - Leeds & Bradford

Dragons

D ragons are nasty
R oar loudly
A ngry dragons
G rumpy animals
O rdinary they are not
N asty animals
S tay far away from them!

Max Dickinson (6)
Churwell Primary School, Morley

Dragons

D angerous and terrifying
R oar loudly, yes
A ngry they are
G orgeous they are not
O ften horrible!
N othing they know is good
S tay away!

Alicia Patnelli (6)
Churwell Primary School, Morley

My First Acrostic - Leeds & Bradford

Dragons

D ragons are dangerous
R avenous and breathe fire
A ngry dragons
G rumpy animals
O rdinary they are not
N asty creatures
S tay far away!

Brandon Johnson (6)
Churwell Primary School, Morley

Dragons

D ragons are scary
R oar so loudly
A re very scary
G row so much
O dd creatures
N ever go near them
S cary.

Jacob Thewlis (5)
Churwell Primary School, Morley

My First Acrostic - Leeds & Bradford

Dragons

D istinctive dragons were fighting
R avenous creatures and scary
A nd they're not nice but terrifying
G obble you up, they would like to
O dd to people, yes they are
N on-fiction, they are not
S tay away, yes!

Sofia Downie Hullah (6)
Churwell Primary School, Morley

Dragons

D angerous creatures
R avenous giants
A ble to gobble you up
G laring his eyes
O bey or he will eat you
N asty big wings
S uper sharp teeth.

Curtis Fox (5)
Churwell Primary School, Morley

My First Acrostic - Leeds & Bradford

Dragons

D angerous creatures
R oaring loudly
A ngry
G igantic
O ften horrible
N ever near them
S tay away

Matilda Peat (5)
Churwell Primary School, Morley

Dragons

D o not go near them
R un away
A nger people
G oogly eyes
O ften scary
N ever go near them
S ometimes they are nasty.

Elizabeth Ketteringham (6)
Churwell Primary School, Morley

My First Acrostic - Leeds & Bradford

Dragons

D angerous dragons fight a lot
R oar terror all the time
A nd eat people
G reedy animals
O ften mean
N ot nice things
S uch mean things.

Ellie Fox (6)
Churwell Primary School, Morley

Dragon

D angerous dragons
R oaring loudly
A nd eating people
G rumpy animals
O rdinary they are not
N asty creatures they can be
S tay away.

Lydia Gill (6)
Churwell Primary School, Morley

My First Acrostic - Leeds & Bradford

Dragons

D ragons are fierce
R avenous creatures they are
A re you afraid?
G et out of here before he eats you!
O ften all the other animals are afraid
N ever anger a dragon
S ee them roar!

Meena Blair (6)
Churwell Primary School, Morley

Dragons

D ragons are dangerous
R un for your life
A ngry creatures
G reedy animals
O bey them
N asty animals
S tay away!

Bethany Allen (6)
Churwell Primary School, Morley

My First Acrostic - Leeds & Bradford

Growing

G rowing plants is fun
R oses are red
O ranges are sweet
W heat is in the ground
I vy grows from the ground
N ettles aren't nice
G rass grows from the ground.

Aishah Hussain (6)
Lapage Primary School, Bradford

Growing

G rowing flowers taller and taller
R oses are red
O range coloured flowers
W ater is needed
I nside a pot
N ice and clean are
G rowing flowers.

Malikah Ahmed (6)
Lapage Primary School, Bradford

My First Acrostic - Leeds & Bradford

Growing

G rowing flowers and plants
R oses growing more and more
O range flowers are growing
W ater all flowers
I nside in pots
N eeds some seeds
G rowing up all.

Tashnia Begum (6)
Lapage Primary School, Bradford

Growing

G rowing a flower
R oses are flowers
O ranges are a kind of fruit
W ater a flower
I vy grass
N ettles aren't nice
G rass grows from a seed.

Zanab Razwan (6)
Lapage Primary School, Bradford

My First Acrostic - Leeds & Bradford

Growing

G roceries can be vegetables
R oses are red
O range is a fruit
W ater is needed for flowers
I vy is a plant
N ettles are not nice
G rass growing tall

Qurratulayn Kazmi (6)
Lapage Primary School, Bradford

Growing

G rowing is about flowers
R oses are brilliant and you need to respect them
O ranges are fruit that you grow
W ater is taken
I am growing flowers
N ext we put in seeds
G rass grows.

Amaan Ali Maryam (5)
Lapage Primary School, Bradford

My First Acrostic - Leeds & Bradford

Growing

G rowing flower
R oses are red
O ranges are nice
W ater is for people and grass
I t needs sun
N ow we need to plant the flower
G rowing flowers is fun.

Loeeza Maryam (5)
Lapage Primary School, Bradford

Growing

G rowing flowers
R oses are red
O range coloured flowers
W ater is good for flowers
I vy outside in a pot
N ettles
G row.

Afia Yasmin Khan (6)
Lapage Primary School, Bradford

My First Acrostic - Leeds & Bradford

Spring

S un is shining
P eople in the park
R ed roses growing
I feel happy
N ice smells
G reen grass grows.

Liam Ralph (6)
Oakwood Primary School, Leeds

Spring

S pring is here
P itter-patter of warm rain on the roof
R oses are growing
I n spring flowers bloom
N ice sun is out today
G reen, lovely green has come to stay.

Shyla Keeble (6)
Oakwood Primary School, Leeds

My First Acrostic - Leeds & Bradford

Spring

S pring is here
P retty daisies
R ed roses growing in spring
I like spring
N ice-looking flowers
G reen grass growing.

Billy Griffin (6)
Oakwood Primary School, Leeds

Spring

S pring is lovely
P retty flowers growing
R ed roses
I n spring flowers are growing
N ice pretty flowers blooming
G reen, lovely green has come to stay.

Ibrahim Mohammed (6)
Oakwood Primary School, Leeds

My First Acrostic - Leeds & Bradford

Spring

S pring has come to stay
P itter-patter of warm rain on the roof
R oses are growing in gardens
I n the spring flowers grow
N ice gorgeous flowers
G reen growing grass.

Paige Smith (6)
Oakwood Primary School, Leeds

Spring

S pring is nice

P ansies are blooming

R ed roses growing

I n spring all the plants need sun and water

N ectar is very good

G reen, lovely green.

Ella McNalus (5)
Oakwood Primary School, Leeds

My First Acrostic - Leeds & Bradford

Spring

S pring is bright
P ink roses are pretty
R oses are pretty
I n fields there are daffodils
N ests up in trees
G ardens with roses.

Aaron Pitts-Smith (6)
Oakwood Primary School, Leeds

Spring

Spring is here
Pitter-patter of warm rain
Roses growing
In blooming roses
Now grass has come to stay
Grass is growing huge.

Zeshan Aziz
Oakwood Primary School, Leeds

My First Acrostic - Leeds & Bradford

Spring

S pring is nice
P itter-patter of warm rain
R ed roses growing in spring
I n spring beautiful flowers grow
N ice flowers blooming
G reen, lovely green has come to stay.

Farai Kavuru (6)
Oakwood Primary School, Leeds

Myself

H arry
A ngry
R ight in maths
R ed is my favourite colour
Y ellow is the table I work on

E vil
M ean
M ad
O bsessed with action movies
T earful
T ired all the time.

Harry Emmott (7)
SS Peter & Paul RC Primary School, Yeadon

My First Acrostic - Leeds & Bradford

Play Time

P acks of people running out to play
L ovely games going on
A nice break from work
Y ummy, yummy fruit

T ime to play tig
I love my play time
M y friend and I like to play army
E very day the play times are brilliant.

William Davy (7)
SS Peter & Paul RC Primary School, Yeadon

Myself

A lways helpful
D ecent I am
A lways a great artist
N ice
N etball is fun
A lways have the answers in my head.

Adanna Okonofua (6)
SS Peter & Paul RC Primary School, Yeadon

My First Acrostic - Leeds & Bradford

Myself

J am I like
O bedient
S ometimes silent
E xciting
P lay well!
H iding

L ovely
A ngry sometimes
N osy
G lad
L eaping
E xterminating
Y our friend

Who am I?

Joseph Langley (7)
SS Peter & Paul RC Primary School, Yeadon

Myself

J umpy boy
A crobatic gym boy
C ool boy I am
K ick well. I am a top striker.

Jack Hazlegreaves (7)
SS Peter & Paul RC Primary School, Yeadon

My First Acrostic - Leeds & Bradford

Myself

B eautiful
E xciting
T all
H elpful
A lways nice
N aughty
Y oung.

Bethany Broadbent (6)
SS Peter & Paul RC Primary School, Yeadon

Play Time

P eople play outside with me, we
L augh and play all day
A nywhere I go there's a friend for
Y ou playing hopscotch, hopping away

T ime to go, bye, bye, bye
I miss you playing outside
M e and you had a great time
E xcited for the next time.

May Gavin (7)
SS Peter & Paul RC Primary School, Yeadon

My First Acrostic - Leeds & Bradford

Myself

N ice
I nteresting
A mazing
M ad
H elpful and happy

W onderful girl
A lways sensible
Y oung.

Niamh Way (7)
SS Peter & Paul RC Primary School, Yeadon

Myself

H appy
O bsessed
L ovely
L eaping
Y oung

M ad
I nteresting
F riendly
S ensible
U ntidy
D elightful.

Holly Mifsud (7)
SS Peter & Paul RC Primary School, Yeadon

My First Acrostic - Leeds & Bradford

Myself

R estless
O ften play Star Wars
R easonable
Y oung boy.

Rory Folan (6)
SS Peter & Paul RC Primary School, Yeadon

Ebony Clark

E very day as sweet as can be
B ony, but long hair
O thers respect her always
N ever naughty in school
Y et fair, tiny face.

C rystal clear eyes
L ovely chatty lips
A nd tiny, delicate hands
R are-shaped body
K ind, loving and a little bit beautiful.

Ebony Clark (6)
St Anthony's Catholic Primary School, Beeston

My First Acrostic - Leeds & Bradford

Me

C aitlin is my name and I am six years old
A nd I don't like baths but do like horses
I n the living room the only thing I like to do is watch TV
T hen Mummy turns it off again and makes me eat my tea
L aughing and playing makes me feel good
I have a pet rabbit called Bunny, she lives in her house of wood
N ight comes and it is time to brush my teeth, and go to sleep.

Caitlin Deacon (6)
St Anthony's Catholic Primary School, Beeston

Elliot

E arly in the morning
L eaving for school
L earning all day
I s so cool
O ut in the playground talking to friends
T elling them about my weekend.

Elliot O'Reilly (7)
St Anthony's Catholic Primary School, Beeston

My First Acrostic - Leeds & Bradford

Millie

M illie is my puppy dog
I n the garden she likes to play
L ong ears she has
L ong skinny legs
I like to play with her
E ats everything she sees on the floor.

Joshua Staniland (7)
St Anthony's Catholic Primary School, Beeston

All About A Princess

P retty every day

R eally sweet

I ncredible to see

N ice to see once you meet her

C ool to see when she comes to play

E very day she comes out to play

S ensible when royal families come to stay

S he always plays with her friends.

Émer Thompson (7)
St Anthony's Catholic Primary School, Beeston

My Little Sister Robyn

R elaxing person
O ne little cheeky girl
B eautiful person
Y oung little girl
N oisy always.

Ellie-Anne Thompson (6)
St Anthony's Catholic Primary School, Beeston

Daisy

Daisy is the name of my dog
And she likes to play with frogs
I like her so much
She is really soft to touch
You can never get her to go in her hutch.

Ellie Gawthorpe (6)
St Anthony's Catholic Primary School, Beeston

My First Acrostic - Leeds & Bradford

I Am Evie

E vie is my first name
V ery nice coloured eyes
I am a very, very good girl
E vie is good at reading.

Evie Plews (7)
St Anthony's Catholic Primary School, Beeston

Oliver

O liver is the best name in the world
L assies and lads love it when I make them laugh
I am loveable to everyone I meet
V ery, very freckly is what I am
E verybody thinks I am super, smashing, great
R unning and jumping, I never sit still.

Oliver Spoors (7)
St Anthony's Catholic Primary School, Beeston

My First Acrostic - Leeds & Bradford

Elizabeth

E lizabeth is my name
L ike the Queen
I like riding my bike
Z oom, zoom, zoom, I go on my bike
A bike is what I like
B ing, bam, zibidi, zoom, that's what I do
E very day is a good day to me
T hat is why I am so
H appy!

Elizabeth Todd (7)
St Anthony's Catholic Primary School, Beeston

Clouds

Carefully floating in the sky way up high
Lots of people watch the clouds
Over the buildings they float by
Under the clouds the world goes by
Day or night they move on
Sunshine is out, now behind the clouds it has gone.

Lucas Lee (7)
St Anthony's Catholic Primary School, Beeston

My First Acrostic - Leeds & Bradford

Chester Zoo

C hester Zoo is lots of good fun,
H ungry hippos are big and fat,
E lephants like the water and the sun
S tripy tigers and hairy lions are big cats,
T he chimpanzees jump from tree to tree
E verybody likes to watch the sea lions swim,
R hinos like mud!

Z ebras are black and white,
O rang-utans are orange,
O h what fun I had at the zoo.

Joseph Maloney (7)
St Anthony's Catholic Primary School, Beeston

Ronaldo

Runs as fast as a lion
On the light green grass
Never stopping
Attention, Ronaldo's coming
Look out, he's going to score
Defenders try to tackle him
One kick and it's a goal!

Patrick Hirsch (7)
St Anthony's Catholic Primary School, Beeston

My First Acrostic - Leeds & Bradford

Casey

C uddly and cool
A ctive
S ensitive
E xcited
Y ellow is my favourite colour.

Casey Lee (6)
St Francis' Catholic Primary School, Morley

Patrick

P layful
A ctive
T alk a lot
R ich
I nteresting
C ool
K ick boxing is my favourite sport.

Patrick Richardson (7)
St Francis' Catholic Primary School, Morley

My First Acrostic - Leeds & Bradford

Victoria

V ery nice
I nteresting
C aring
T icklish
O bjective
R ed is my favourite colour
I n the school
A ctive.

Victoria Massey (5)
St Francis' Catholic Primary School, Morley

Lucas

Lucky
Understanding
Cuddly
Active
Silly.

Lucas Ottley (5)
St Francis' Catholic Primary School, Morley

My First Acrostic - Leeds & Bradford

Lauren

L ucky
A ctive
U nique
R eads books
E njoys working
N ice.

Lauren Wilson (5)
St Francis' Catholic Primary School, Morley

Harry

Happy
Active
Run around in a
Rush
Yellow is my favourite colour.

Harry Bussey (5)
St Francis' Catholic Primary School, Morley

My First Acrostic - Leeds & Bradford

Fawn

F abulous
A ctive
W onderful
N atters.

Fawn Goodwin (7)
St Francis' Catholic Primary School, Morley

Olivia

O utstanding
L ovely
I ntelligent
V ery good at maths
I 'm a nice girl and
A ctive.

Olivia Turner (7)
St Francis' Catholic Primary School, Morley

My First Acrostic - Leeds & Bradford

Fletcher

F unny
L ikes games
E nergetic
T rouble
C ares for others
H appy
E asy-going
R ugby player.

Fletcher Trueman (6)
St Francis' Catholic Primary School, Morley

Amy

A mazing
M ight be a popstar
Y ellow is my favourite colour.

Amy Atkin (7)
St Francis' Catholic Primary School, Morley

My First Acrostic - Leeds & Bradford

Corey

C ool Corey
O n the football pitch
R uns
E verywhere
Y es, a goal.

Corey Franks (6)
Shadwell Primary School, Shadwell

Charles

C aring
H onest
A nd
R eally
L ucky and
E xcited at
S am's house.

Charles Fenwick (5)
Shadwell Primary School, Shadwell

My First Acrostic - Leeds & Bradford

Polly

P retty Polly is
O ften pretty and a
L ovely cute friend she
L ikes playing with
Y ou.

Polly Wearmouth (6)
Shadwell Primary School, Shadwell

Ruby

R uby is kind and
U nderstanding and
B eautiful, likes
Y ellow lollies.

Ruby Fullman (5)
Shadwell Primary School, Shadwell

Maddie

Marvellous Maddie is
Afraid and
Dazzling and loves to
Dance. She
Is kind as well and she is
Exciting.

Maddie Wood (6)
Shadwell Primary School, Shadwell

Harry

H appy Harry
A lways
R uns
R ound the
Y ard.

Harry Fenwick (5)
Shadwell Primary School, Shadwell

My First Acrostic - Leeds & Bradford

Megan Davis

M arvellous Megan is
E xtremely kind
G reat at drawing
A nd very good at not being
N aughty and

D aft
A t drawing and
V ery good at silly words
I 'm good at being a friend
S o be my friend.

Megan Davis (6)
Shadwell Primary School, Shadwell

Daniel

D aft Daniel is
A lways
N ice and
I s very silly and
E njoys
L ovely tig.

Daniel Coates (6)
Shadwell Primary School, Shadwell

My First Acrostic - Leeds & Bradford

Maisie Hanna

M arvellous Maisie
A lways at school makes
I nteresting egg pictures and is a
S uper girl
I n the classroom she is
E xcellent at everything!

H as a big smile
A nd is
N ice not
N aughty
A nd always happy.

Maisie Hanna Wood
Shadwell Primary School, Shadwell

Imogen Bowman

I ntelligent Imogen is
M arvellous
O r
G reat
E xtremely beautiful and
N ever naughty

B eautiful Imogen always
O n time
W ill
M ake you smile
A nd is
N ever unkind.

Imogen Bowman (6)
Shadwell Primary School, Shadwell

My First Acrostic - Leeds & Bradford

Amber

A lways smiley and
M arvellous Amber is
B eautiful and makes really good
E gg pictures and does really good handwriting, it's
R eally great.

Amber Webb (6)
Shadwell Primary School, Shadwell

Ali Naim

A mazing Ali
L ikes
I ce cream

N ot good at colouring
A li
I s
M arvellous.

Ali Naim
Shadwell Primary School, Shadwell

My First Acrostic - Leeds & Bradford

Young Writers Information

We hope you have enjoyed reading this book - and that you will continue to enjoy it in the coming years.

If you like reading and writing poetry drop us a line, or give us a call, and we'll send you a free information pack.

Alternatively if you would like to order further copies of this book or any of our other titles, then please give us a call or log onto our website at www.youngwriters.co.uk.

Young Writers Information
Remus House
Coltsfoot Drive
Peterborough
PE2 9JX
(01733) 890066